KOKOP____

COOK BOOK

by
James and Carol Cunkle

**GOLDEN
WEST ☼
PUBLISHERS**

Cover design and all text illustrations by James R. Cunkle.

Special thanks to Steven A. LeBlanc *(The Mimbres People: Ancient Pueblo Painters of the American Southwest)* and the Maxwell Museum in Albuquerque for their assistance in this research.

Back cover photo of authors by Cheryl Miller.

Dedication

To our daughters.
Whose beauty, grace and spirit
give meaning and enrichment
to our lives

> **Note:** All plants listed as edible in this book should be picked and used only by those who are thoroughly familiar with making appropriate plant selections. Check with authorities prior to picking any wild plants so as not to violate any federal, state, or local laws.

Library of Congress Cataloguing in Publication Data
Cunkle, James R
      Kokopelli's Cook Book / by James and Carol Cunkle
        p.   cm.
   Includes index
   ISBN 1-885590-24-5
   1. Indian cookery.   2. Indians of North America—Food
   3. Kokopelli (Pueblo deity)   I. Cunkle, Carol
TX715.C96273   1997   97-40447
641.59'297—dc21   CIP

Printed in the United States of America

10th printing © 2004

Information in this book is deemed to be authentic and accurate by authors and publisher. However, they disclaim any liability incurred in connection with the use of information appearing in this book.

Golden West Publishers, Inc.
4113 N. Longview Ave.
Phoenix, AZ 85014, USA
(800) 658-5830

For free sample recipes and complete Table of Contents for every Golden West cookbook, visit our website: **goldenwestpublishers.com**

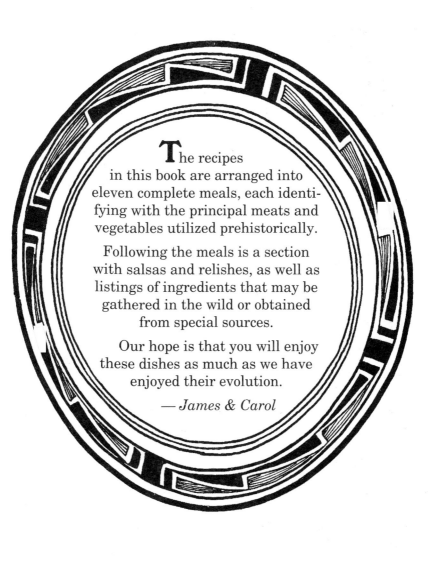

The recipes
in this book are arranged into
eleven complete meals, each identifying with the principal meats and
vegetables utilized prehistorically.

Following the meals is a section
with salsas and relishes, as well as
listings of ingredients that may be
gathered in the wild or obtained
from special sources.

Our hope is that you will enjoy
these dishes as much as we have
enjoyed their evolution.

— James & Carol

Table of Contents

Introduction

For nearly a decade Carol (my wife and partner) and I have been directing the excavations and research at Raven Site Ruins, a prehistoric pueblo in east-central Arizona operating under the auspices of the White Mountain Archaeological Center.

Our research at Raven Site has taught us that one can learn a great deal from the vessels produced by prehistoric Indians. Careful study of the pottery itself, the methods used to produce it, and the size and shape of the items yields an enormous amount of data. For example, at Raven Site we excavate very few plates. Most of the ceramics uncovered are either large storage jars or serving bowls. This tends to indicate that most of the meals served centuries ago at this site were soups and stews.

Furthermore, it is impossible to ignore the intricate and often colorful designs found on the ceramics excavated at Raven Site Ruins and other sites across the Southwest. Nearly one thousand years ago, Mimbres potters created the remarkable designs that grace the pages of this volume. The designs on prehistoric pottery may suggest not only the purpose of each vessel, but perhaps, more importantly, when that vessel was to be used. Ceremonies honoring the dead, prayers for bountiful crops, and celebrations of the hunt all called for a unique vessel bearing its own unique design. Just as important as the walls of the pueblo itself, the designs and distinctive wear marks of the ceramics are keys to uncovering the mysteries of the prehistoric peoples.

Archaeological and anthropological research also reveals what the prehistoric peoples ate. Evidence of crops, seeds, and animal bones reveal bountiful meals—at least by prehistoric standards. Rabbits and antelope appear to have been two of the most commonly consumed animals, followed by turkey and dog. Moreover, corn, beans and squash appear to have been the principal crops. The simple combination of corn and beans provided most of the essential amino acids and enzymes necessary for a balanced diet.

To bring to life the flavors of the past, Carol spent years reinventing meals of the past for today's hungry researchers and visitors at Raven Site. A few years ago, we discovered some beans sitting inside a prehistoric bowl in a dry cave not far from the dig site. A sample was sent to researchers in Tucson, Arizona, in an attempt to preserve the original genetic stock. We also decided to plant a few. For eons those beans must have patiently awaited moisture and sunlight because before long they sprouted and grew!

It was not long thereafter that we planted an entire ethnobotanical garden at Raven Site using seeds the Native Americans traditionally grew. Visitors to the site enjoyed wandering between the rows and Carol continued to experiment with the harvest, creating new recipes from traditional yields like corn, beans, squash and chiles.

"Kokopelli's Kitchen," a gourmet/specialty line of fine food products, is the result of these early culinary experiments. These splendid products help fund the continuing research at Raven Site Ruins. Through their development, we have enjoyed experiencing firsthand the influence of the varied and diverse cultures of the Southwest, including the Spanish, Mexican Indians, and Anglo Pioneers. All have left their imprint on the people, the landscape and the foods.

A final note: As some prehistoric ingredients are no longer available, we have adapted a few of the recipes to modern times. In addition, contemporary tastes and dietary habits of our own cultures demand some slight alterations. With every adaptation we have made every effort to remain true to the original version of the Native recipe. A resource page in the back of the book has been included to help enthusiasts locate some of the more unique and special ingredients.

The Mimbres Images

All of the images illustrated in this volume were painted virtually a thousand years ago on the insides of ceramic bowls. These bowls were then buried with the dead in an elaborate ritual. The prehistoric people who painted these wonderful images were called the Mimbres and they lived in the area of the Southwest that is now southern New Mexico.

The talented Mimbres painters who created these fantastic illustrations lived between A.D. 1000 and A.D. 1280 in the area that is now called the Mimbres Valley. "Mimbres" means "willow" in Spanish. When the early conquistadors marched into what is now the state of New Mexico they saw a valley and a tiny river edged by willow trees and they named the valley "Mimbres". No Mimbres peoples inhabited the valley when the Spanish marched by. All of the prehistoric people had long since moved.

There is a lot of speculation as to where these people went after they left the valley that they had inhabited for so many centuries. There is an equal amount of conjecture as to from where they originally came. Pottery is often an excellent indicator revealing clues to the origins and movements of groups of people in the prehistoric Southwest.

They grew corn, beans, squash, amaranth and many crops that we no longer cultivate. They also hunted and fished.

The typical prehistoric Mimbres village would hold little interest today even to the archaeologist except for one very important contribution made ages ago by these talented people. They painted figurative images on their ceramics. Unlike the Mimbres' remarkable ceramic designs, their buildings are not spectacular like the grandiose structures at Chaco Canyon. Villages were small, usually with no more than thirty or forty rectangular rooms. Even the ceramics were poorly made, thick, poorly polished and fired haphazardly.

Where the Mimbres migrated to after they left the Mimbres Valley is also a bit of a mystery. The most plausible explanation is that these people assimilated with the other indigenous peoples

of northern Mexico, specifically the residents of the ruin of Paquime and its extensive outliers. When they moved they seem to have left the practice of burying these figurative vessels behind. In no other part of the Southwest was this practice repeated in later times nor has this ritual been discovered in any other area than the Mimbres Valley.

All of the prehistoric Mimbres bowls illustrated in this volume were buried with the dead. The bowls were placed over the face of the deceased and the bottom of the bowl was broken, punched out either by a small stone or a sharp instrument such as a bone awl. This "kill hole" is clearly visible in nearly all of the examples presented in this study. In many cases the kill hole obliterates important elements of the depiction. Interestingly, the piece of ceramic that was punched out of the bottom of the bowl is never recovered during the excavation of the vessel. This sherd of ceramic was probably carried off by those persons doing the burying. Most researchers explain the nature of the kill hole as a ritual breaking of the bowl so that the spirit of the bowl will travel with the deceased to the next world. As the body is absent of life, and the spirit of the body has departed, so must the spirit of the vessel be freed. This ritual breaking of the vessel frees the spirit of the bowl. In the mythology of the prehistoric Mimbres all things have a spirit. The animals, the plants, the mountains and skies, the rocks and rivers all possess a spirit, a consciousness beyond this, the fourth world.

New research has provided a second possible explanation as to the nature of the kill hole found on Mimbres bowls. The rim of the bowl when placed over the face of the deceased creates the horizon of the earth and the body of the inverted bowl simulates the dome of the underworld sky. The images painted in the bowl create a world within the dome with the facsimiles of life, of myth, and of legend. The hole is punched into the top of the dome creating the sky window, or eye of God, the sipapu, the doorway into the next level of being. Through this sipapu the deceased will travel up into the next world, just as the people in the beginning emerged from below the earth up through the navel of the world from the third world below into this fourth world of existence. Many of the

Mimbres bowls illustrate a swift near the kill hole. The high flying swift is believed to be the guide who leads the spirit of the deceased up and through the sky window into the next world.

When viewing these remarkable and sometimes confusing images a thousand years removed from their making it is often a tremendous challenge to glean the meaning behind the objects, animals and people portrayed. It would seem that the context of the image, i.e. the interior of a painted bowl which was buried with the dead, and this extremely nuclear use and seemingly singular purpose should be reflected in the image displayed. But after studying thousands of these figurative paintings no "death" context seems to be readily apparent. Many of the animals that were painted do have Underworld connotations but many others do not. Certainly scenes of hunting may have been buried with a hunter or a member of a particular clan may have been buried with an image depicting the associated animals of that clan group. Proving any association of the image on the grave good vessel and the deceased is in most cases not possible because of the poor provenance of the vessels. If the skeletal remains had been preserved and curated along with the associated vessel it indeed would be possible to research whether or not the deceased was a hunter, child, shaman, potter, specialist, generalist, etc., and then a comparison could have been made to the image on the bowls and the archaeologist could have tested this probability.

However, an association between the images on the bowls and the people they were buried with may not directly occur. Many of the images are joyful, even humorous and they abundantly illustrate the rich mythology of the Mimbres. Many of the bowls were used for many years before they were buried with the deceased. Wear patterns are often evident on the surfaces of the vessels.

The Mimbres Indians were a small group of the greater Mogollon Culture from a small area of the prehistoric Southwest. These bowls were produced and buried for only about 200 years, even so, these images are some of the best evidence that remains of the rich mythology of the prehistoric Southwest Indians. These fantastic paintings are virtual time capsules, windows to peek through and snoop into the mythology of prehistory.

Kokopelli's
Cook Book

RECIPES

Antelope on a Cliff

This beautiful bowl was skillfully painted using the usually geometric elements as landscape. The pronghorn antelope balances gracefully on the edge. Entire herds of these animals were driven into stone catchpens for a sacrificial death. Select organs were ritualistically removed while the animals were still alive.

Although difficult to find commercially, wild game is a real treat. Elk is by far the best red meat you will ever taste and is almost always tender and delicious no matter which cut you try. Wild game must be properly dressed and aged for the meat to be at its best. Prehistorically, the Indians of the Southwest killed elk, deer and antelope by driving whole herds over cliffs. Special walls of stone were constructed to force the animals into the abyss. After the kill, prayers and offerings were made to the animals, thanking them for sacrificing themselves to feed the Pueblo peoples.

Grilled Elk, Venison or Beef

6 (8-10 ounce) steaks cut 1" thick
mesquite pods

Prepare *Juniper Marinade,* add steaks, cover and refrigerate for 4 hours, turning once. Reserve remaining marinade.

Add the mesquite pods to coals five minutes before grilling. Grill steaks five to ten minutes per side, brushing once with marinade after turning. Serve with *Juniper Marinade Sauce* on the side. Serves 4 to 6.

Note: Consuming wild game cooked rare is not recommended.

Juniper Marinade

1 T. juniper berries
1/4 cup vegetable oil
1 cup dry red wine
3/4 t. salt
1/2 t. pepper

1/2 t. onion powder
1/4 t. hot pepper sauce
1/8 t. liquid smoke
2 t. Worcestershire sauce

Place a clean towel over berries and crush with a heavy skillet or mallet. Combine with balance of ingredients in a glass, ceramic or stainless steel container.

Juniper Marinade Sauce

Place remaining *Juniper Marinade* in a saucepan and combine with the **1 cup beef broth**. Simmer for 15 minutes, or until liquid is reduced to half. Strain. Yields 2 1/2 cups.

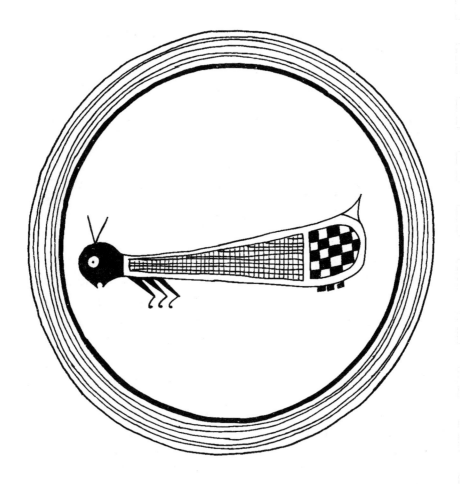

Locusts

Locusts and other insects were very commonly depicted by the Mimbres artists. Notice the checkerboard pattern on the abdomen. The checkerboard pattern symbolized the Milky Way or "starry sky".

The Indians of the Andes have been growing potatoes for over 4000 years. After the Spanish conquest of Central and South America the potato was introduced into Europe where it quickly replaced many of the cereal grains. The potato became an important staple in the Old World. Sir Francis Drake introduced the potato to England and Ireland after A.D. 1580.

Skillet Potatoes

6 medium-sized russet potatoes, unpeeled
2 T. lemon juice
2 T. canola oil
1 t. salt
1/2 t. freshly ground pepper
1 t. pure chile powder
2 T. chopped fresh cilantro

Scrub potatoes and slice thin. Cover potatoes with salted water to which lemon juice has been added. Refrigerate for one hour. Drain well. Toss potatoes with oil, salt, pepper, and chile powder. Heat a large cast iron skillet on grill. Allow the skillet (ungreased) to become very hot. Place potatoes in the skillet (do not turn) for 4 minutes. With a long handled spatula, turn the potatoes and continue frying for an additional 6 minutes. Garnish with cilantro. Serves 4 to 6.

These potatoes may also be fried in the oven:

Preheat oven to 425°. Place cast iron skillet in oven for 15 minutes to heat thoroughly. Remove pan from oven and follow instructions above, allowing 15 minutes per side.

Caution: Skillet handle will be very hot! Use thick oven mitts.

Butterfly Men

Human and animal combinations abound in Mimbres art. The appendage on the backs of these men are identified as butterfly wings by the white margin dots. The outlined crosses represent a large star or planet.

Squash has been a principle crop of the Pueblo peoples for centuries. The Hopi and Zuni personify and impersonate the squash plants in their Katsina dances. According to the Pueblo mythologies, these Katsinas bring health, long life, fertility and rain to the villages. Among the Hopi, the chief Katsina of the Pumpkin Clan is the Squash Katsina or "Patung".

Squash Medley

2 T. olive oil
1 medium yellow summer squash,
    cut diagonally in 1/4" slices
1 medium zucchini, cut diagonally in 1/4" slices
1/2 cup seeded and julienned red bell pepper
1 small green chile pepper, seeded and julienned
1 small onion, cut in 1/4" slices
1 t. salt
1/2 t. freshly ground pepper
1/4 t. dried dill weed or 1 t. fresh dill weed, snipped
2 T. olive oil
4 T. grated Parmesan cheese

In a medium-sized skillet, heat oil. Add the vegetables and stir fry over medium high heat for approximately 10 minutes or until semi-soft. Add salt, pepper, dill and then toss. Sprinkle Parmesan over the top. Serve immediately. Serves 4-6.

Serving suggestion: Garnish individual serving plates with fresh tomato wedges.

Butterfly

Butterflies are female symbols representing fertility. The flight of the butterfly is similar to the flight of the spirits of the ancestors. Traditional Hopis still respect butterflies, as they may represent a departed loved one.

Native Americans of the Southwest raised dozens of varieties of corn. Blue corn actually ranges in color from pale blue to almost black. Researchers believe that blue corn has more nutritional value than other varieties.

Blue Corn Cakes
with Wild Blueberry Sauce

1 cup all-purpose or
   enriched white flour
1 cup stone-ground
   blue cornmeal
3 t. baking powder
1/4 t. salt
1/2 cup sugar
1 t. vanilla
3 eggs, well beaten
1 1/2 cups milk, room
   temperature
4 T. melted butter

Preheat oven to 350°. Sift together the first five ingredients. Set aside. Mix together the vanilla, eggs, milk and butter. Combine the dry ingredients with the liquid ingredients. Grease and lightly flour a 9 x 12 baking dish. Pour the batter into dish and bake for 30 to 40 minutes or until a toothpick inserted into center comes out clean.

Immediately upon removing the cake from the oven, pierce the top surface with a fork. Spoon the **Wild Blueberry Sauce** over the top. Serve warm or cold with ice cream or top with a dollop of whipped cream. Serves 4 to 6.

Wild Blueberry Sauce

2 cups (1 pint) wild blueberries
   (or huckleberries)
1 cup water
1/2 cup sugar
1/4 t. salt
2 T. cornstarch
4 T. water
1 T. butter

Combine the berries, water, sugar and salt in a medium saucepan. Bring mixture to a boil and simmer gently for 15 minutes. While simmering, mash the berries slightly with a potato masher. Mix the cornstarch into water. With the blueberries still simmering, slowly stir in the cornstarch mixture. Continue to stir for at least two minutes. Remove from heat and stir in butter.

Frog

Frogs are water symbols and associated with the creation myth. *When The People lived below in the third world they had webbed digits and tails. They emerged through the sipapu onto this, the fourth world, and blinked in the sunlight. The Warrior Twins came along and separated their webbed digits and cut off their tails and they became human.* The transition from tadpole to frog mirrors this mythology. The grid dot pattern shown on the frog represents "corn."

Frogs, clams, fish and snails were prehistoric delicacies. Archaeological sites in the Southwest are rich with the small bones and shells of these aquatic animals.

Frog Legs

18 pairs small frog legs, fresh or frozen
milk
all-purpose or enriched white flour
salt
pepper
1/2 cup unsalted butter
1/4 cup olive oil
2 cloves garlic, minced
1 shallot, minced
1/4 cup white wine
1/4 cup chicken broth
1 tablespoon chopped parsley
1 lemon, wedged

Clean and separate frog legs. Place legs in a dish, cover with milk and refrigerate several hours. Drain. Roll legs in flour seasoned with the salt and pepper. In a heavy skillet melt 1/4 cup of butter and olive oil over medium heat. Add frog legs and sauté until golden brown. Transfer to a warmed platter. Wipe out skillet, return to medium high heat and melt the remaining butter. Add garlic, shallot, wine and broth. Sauté until just heated through. Pour sauce over frog legs. Sprinkle top with parsley, garnish with lemon wedges and serve immediately. Serves 4-6.

Man with Snakes

The man in this painting is handling two snakes and one more waits in a basket. His face is painted white representing death or dealing with death. Mimbres painters were very specific about representing rattles of poisonous rattlesnakes. The snakes here are not rattlesnakes.

The Hopi Indians of Arizona perform a sacred ceremony every February. Beans are planted in special pots within the kiva and are tenderly cared for by the Powamu Katsinas. Quick germination and growth ensures an abundant harvest.

Black Bean Cakes
with Sour Cream Sauce

3/4 cup chicken broth or water
3/4 cup yellow cornmeal
2 cups cooked black beans
1 t. salt
1/2 t. freshly ground pepper
1/4 t. cumin
1/2 t. Mexican oregano
dash of hot pepper sauce
1 T. olive or vegetable oil
1 green onion, cut in half lengthwise then thinly
    sliced (include the tops)
1/2 t. minced garlic clove
2 T. olive or vegetable oil

In a medium saucepan bring the broth (or water) to a boil. Add the cornmeal, stirring constantly until thickened. Reduce heat and continue stirring and cooking for 2 minutes. Remove from heat. Add all other ingredients (except the last 2 tablespoons of oil) and combine thoroughly. Heat 2 T. of oil in a skillet. Form the bean mixture into cakes. Fry until golden on both sides. Serve immediately with **Sour Cream Sauce**. Serves 4 to 6.

Sour Cream Sauce

1 cup sour cream
1/2 t. salt
1/2 t. white pepper
1/2 t. onion powder
dash hot pepper sauce

Combine all ingredients. Serve at room temperature garnished with snipped fresh **chives**.

Hummingbirds Around a Flower

This extraordinarily detailed image is one of the finest representations of Mimbres art known. Notice that the white background represents the four directions or fourth world as do many other ceramic paintings. The hummingbird probably held a unique symbolic meaning for the Mimbreños similar to that of the butterfly.

Corn and beans were the two primary crops of the prehistoric Indians of the Southwest. These two staples in combination provide nearly all of the essential amino acids and enzymes for a balanced diet.

Succotash

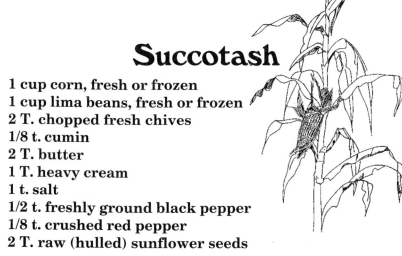

1 cup corn, fresh or frozen
1 cup lima beans, fresh or frozen
2 T. chopped fresh chives
1/8 t. cumin
2 T. butter
1 T. heavy cream
1 t. salt
1/2 t. freshly ground black pepper
1/8 t. crushed red pepper
2 T. raw (hulled) sunflower seeds

In boiling water, cook the corn and beans to desired tenderness. Drain. Add all other ingredients except the sunflower seeds. Cook over medium heat until the liquid is all but absorbed. Garnish with the sunflower seeds. Serves 4-6.

Serving suggestion: Garnish each serving plate with fresh edible flower blossoms (see page 105).

Antelope, Fish & Flowers

This bold bowl illustrates many naturalistic and symbolic elements. Antelope are perched atop fish and nearby, large blossoms bloom. These are probably representations of the tobacco flower. Notice the outlined crosses. This symbol represents a large star or planet and in some cases the MesoAmerican god Quetzacoatl.

The Pueblo people grew melons that were introduced from South America thousands of years ago. The fruit was dried in long spiral strips and eaten as a treat throughout the winter months.

Minted Melon

In individual glass bowls arrange three or more of the following melons cut into balls, cubes, slices or a combination of shapes.

- **watermelon**
- **cantaloupe**
- **honeydew**
- **casaba**
- **Persian**
- **Crenshaw**

Squeeze a little **lime juice** over the melon. Garnish with sprigs of **fresh mint.** Serve with cookies that have chocolate mint coating or filling.

How to choose a ripe melon: Melons are best if they have matured on the vine. The navel scar of the stem end should be slightly sunken and well calloused. Some of the softer rind melons such as cantaloupes have a slight fragrance and the ends should be somewhat soft when pressed. In watermelons, look for "sugar seepage" on the stem end and rind scarring. This "sugar seepage" will be dark and rather crystalline.

Four Turkeys

Turkeys were used for food and feathers and were also sacrificed and buried in the floor to dedicate a new pueblo room. The center diamond on the turkeys' bodies indicates the "center." Turkeys have no other directional significance. The white space around the birds is interpreted by some researchers to represent turkey eggs. The large fantail of the turkey is the single representational element necessary to indicate "turkey" in Mimbres mythology and symbolism.

Turkeys, dogs and parrots were the three domesticated animals of the prehistoric Southwest. Turkeys may have domesticated themselves, as the birds will not leave a food source even if threatened. The Pueblo Indians may have caged and started raising the birds simply to keep them out of their gardens.

Turkey Chili

2 T. olive or vegetable oil
2 pounds ground turkey
1 large onion, coarsely chopped
1 clove garlic, minced
1 t. salt
1/2 t. pepper
1/4 t. sugar
2 T. pure chile powder, mild or hot*
1/2 t. ground cumin
2 t. Mexican oregano
1 bay leaf
1 medium green chile pepper, seeded, coarsely
    chopped
2 cups cooked pinto or kidney beans
2 cups water or chicken broth

Heat oil in a 2-quart saucepan. Add meat, onion and garlic. Brown. Add all other ingredients. Cover and simmer over low heat for 30 minutes. Remove bay leaf and continue cooking uncovered for 30 minutes more. Serves 4-6.

Serving suggestion: Garnish each serving individually with **diced onion, grated Monterey Jack cheese,** and **chopped fresh cilantro.**

*For a much hotter chili, add **1 t. ground chipotle powder** in addition to either mild or hot chile powder. (Chipotle peppers are dried and smoked jalapeños.)

Four Figures

Look carefully at this prehistoric bowl and decide what images you see. Are you sure? Do you see four people with a common circle representing their heads? Most people do at first look. That is because you are looking at the black image, that is, the positive paint. Look at the white, or negative, image and you will see the four ghosts of the people.

Tortillas in one form or another have been the center of the meal throughout the Southwest and MesoAmerica for ages. When we lived with the Maya, Doña Tina would pat out the dough and cook the tortillas on flat rocks while we dined. She could stack them up faster than we could gobble them down.

Flour Tortillas

2 1/2 cups all-purpose or enriched white flour
1 1/2 t. salt
1/2 t baking powder
6 T. lard or vegetable shortening
3/4 cup hot water

In a large bowl, mix together the flour, salt and baking powder. Add the lard and combine thoroughly with your fingertips. Make a depression in the center, add the hot water and continue mixing. Turn out onto a lightly floured work surface and knead until pliable (about five minutes). Cover and allow to rest, refrigerated, for one hour. Divide and shape into 12 balls. With a rolling pin, roll each ball into a 7- or 8-inch circle about 1/8-inch thick. (A tortilla press can be purchased where Mexican and/or gourmet foods are sold).

Heat a large heavy skillet or tortilla griddle over high heat. Cook until tortilla puffs and brown spots appear. Flip over and repeat. To get rid of bubbles after turning, press lightly with your hand protected with a clean kitchen towel or potholder. Keep tortillas warm by wrapping in a clean linen towel or placing in a tortilla warmer. Makes 12 tortillas.

To reheat tortillas:

Microwave: Wrap two tortillas in a paper towel and heat for twenty seconds at a high setting.

Oven: Wrap tortillas in foil and heat for 5 to 10 minutes at 350°.

Two Locusts and a Corn Stalk

Plants were rarely illustrated by Mimbres painters. This painting of a cornstalk complete with roots and tassels is very uncommon. Locusts and other insects were frequently shown. Corn was the principal cereal grain raised by the Pueblo Indians for centuries.

Corn was originally a small grass which yielded only a few kernels. Over the centuries the Indians selected the best ears to replant the following year. This religious hybridizing resulted in corn eventually becoming the large and succulent ears we enjoy today.

Corn on the Cob

4 to 6 ears freshly picked sweet corn

Yellow corn is more tender and more genuinely sweet when fresh. White corn tends to be consistently sweet but is somewhat starchier.

Boiled: Remove the husks and silk. Drop the corn carefully, one by one, into rapidly boiling water. Continue boiling rapidly for 3 to 5 minutes. To prevent toughness add salt halfway through the cooking process.

Steamed: Remove the husks and silk. Bring the water in the lower part of steamer to a brisk boil. Place corn in perforated top of steamer and set in place over boiling water. Cover and cook 10 minutes or until tender.

Grilled outdoors: Pull down the husks and remove the silk and any damaged portions of the corn. Soak in water for one hour. Drain, pull up the husks and tie the top with a strip of husk or twine. Place ears on a grill over hot coals and slowly roast for 20 to 25 minutes, turning occasionally.

Roasted indoors: Preheat oven to 400°. Remove husks and spread a small amount of butter on corn. Wrap each ear in foil and roast until tender (20 to 25 minutes).

The cooking time for all of these methods will vary depending upon the maturity and variety of corn.

> *For the sweetest, neatest corn eating:* For corn on the cob, use a serrated knife to cut lengthwise through the center of each row of kernels before serving.
>
> For corn off the cob, remove kernels from the cob using a paring knife (do not cut into the cob too deeply), then use the dull edge of the knife to press and squeeze out the remaining heart of the kernels and juice from the cob.

Swifts

These high-flying birds were believed to be the guides that led
the spirit up and through the *sky window* or *sipapu* of the sky
created when a bowl's bottom was punched out during the
burial ceremony. Many examples of Mimbres bowls illustrate
the swift. Notice the wavy line that connects the two birds at
the mouth. This wavy line is believed to have symbolized voice,
song or communication.

Pumpkins were being grown in the Southwest long before the Spanish Conquistadors arrived and were valued not only for their delicious flesh but also for their nutritious seeds. The body of the pumpkin makes a handy cooking or serving pot for soups and stews.

Pumpkin Bread

3 eggs, beaten
1/4 cup sunflower oil
3/4 cup brown sugar, packed
3/4 cup honey
1/2 t. ginger
1/2 t. cinnamon
1/2 t. cardamom
1 1/2 cups pumpkin, canned or freshly cooked
2/3 cup light cream
3 cups all-purpose or enriched white flour
1 1/2 t. baking powder
1 1/2 t. baking soda
1/2 t. salt
3/4 cup coarsely chopped black walnuts or pecans

Preheat oven to 350°. Mix together the first nine ingredients. Sift together the flour, baking powder, baking soda, and salt. Combine with the pumpkin mixture and mix thoroughly. Mix in the nuts. Pour into the two well-greased 5 x 9 loaf pans and bake for 1 hour, or until a toothpick inserted into the center comes out clean. Cool on a wire rack, slice thin and spread with the following *Cream Cheese Spread.* Yields 2 loaves.

Sliced, sugared peaches are a nice accompaniment to serve with this recipe!

Cream Cheese Spread

8 oz. softened cream cheese
1 T. light cream
1/2 t. lemon peel
2 T. honey

Whip all ingredients together until smooth.

Bighorn Sheep

Illustrating the horns of this animal is all that was necessary to represent the concept of the bighorn sheep. Often all of the other graphic elements of the depiction were ignored. This is true of many animals found painted by the Mimbres artists. In the case of the mountain lion, the long tail was the magic element and with the crane it was the bird's long neck.

Prehistorically the bighorn sheep was a sacred animal. It is the totem animal of many of the Hopi and Zuni clans. After A.D. 1500 the Navajo arrived in the Southwest and began to raise sheep and goats which had been introduced by the Spaniards. Lamb is still the principal meat of the Navajo Indians.

Lamb Stew

2 T. olive or vegetable oil
2 pounds boneless lamb, cut into 1-inch cubes
1 leek, coarsely chopped
1 clove garlic, minced
1 1/2 t. salt
1/2 t. freshly ground pepper
1 t. fresh thyme or 1/4 t. dried, ground thyme
2 cups water
2 fresh green chiles, seeded and coarsely chopped
3 medium unpeeled potatoes, cut into 1-inch cubes
1 cup unpeeled yellow squash, cut into 1-inch cubes
3/4 cup corn, fresh or frozen
1 cup water
2 cups coarsely chopped fresh spinach or sorrel

Heat oil in a large saucepan or Dutch oven on medium high heat. Brown half of the meat, onion and garlic, remove and repeat with the second half. Return the first half to the pan and add the salt, pepper, thyme and water. Cover, reduce heat, and simmer for 30 minutes. Add the chiles, potatoes, squash, corn and 1 cup water. Cover and cook 20 minutes or until tender. Add spinach, cover and cook an additional five minutes. Serve in bowls. Serves 4 - 6.

Bird with Fish

This is a delightful illustration of a bird eating fish. The fish can be seen within the bird's belly. It is somewhat difficult to determine what species of bird is shown. Some researchers say that the bird is a turkey, others feel it is a waterfowl.

In the prehistoric Pueblo cultures of the Southwest most of the meals served were stews and soups. This is made apparent by the abundance of bowls used as the principal serving dish and by the almost total lack of flatware. Dumplings made from corn were a common addition to the daily diet.

Corn Dumplings

2 cups all-purpose enriched white flour
4 t. baking powder
2 1/2 t. salt
6 T. yellow cornmeal
1/2 cup vegetable shortening
2 cups corn, fresh or frozen, cooked and mashed
   or whole
1 t. red pepper flakes
1/2 t. ground cumin
1 t. chopped dried parsley or 2 T. chopped fresh
1 t. chopped dried chives or 2 T. chopped fresh
1 cup milk

Sift together flour, baking powder, salt and cornmeal. Work in shortening with fingertips. Add remaining ingredients and mix together. Dough will be stiff. Spoon by tablespoonfuls into simmering broth or gravy. Cover pan and simmer over low heat for 15 minutes. Dumplings will increase in size significantly while cooking. Serves 4 - 6.

Crane Eating Fish

Several prehistoric Mimbres bowls illustrate this exact theme. The fish are shown being swallowed and going down into the belly of the crane. Cranes were underworld figures in Mimbres mythology and often painted in scenes depicting decapitation. The checkerboard pattern represents the Milky Way which is a pathway for the Warrior Twins. Note the checkerboard pattern in the border of the bowl.

Chile peppers originated in South America. Wild capsicums spread throughout MesoAmerica and north into the American Southwest. Chiles were the most common spice used by prehistoric Indians. When Coronado met him, Montezuma was sitting on his throne drinking a concoction of cocoa and chile powder.

Roasted & Stuffed Chile Peppers

12 fresh long green chile peppers
8 oz. softened cream cheese
1 T. fresh chives, snipped

While wearing rubber gloves, puncture the entire length of each chile with the tip of a paring knife. Place chiles close together in a shallow baking pan and broil about 6 inches from the heat. When blistered and browned, turn over, using tongs. Each side should take 3 to 4 minutes. Place the chiles immediately in a tightly covered container (pan, paper or plastic bag) for 15 minutes. This steaming process will allow the skin to be removed easily. While wearing rubber gloves, leave the stem intact and use a sharp knife to slit the chiles from the stem end to the tip along the perforations*. Carefully remove the skin, seeds and membranes.

Mix cream cheese and chives together and spread each chile with 1 tablespoon of the cheese mixture. Again place chiles in a shallow baking pan. Salt lightly. Warm in a 200 degree oven for five minutes. Serves 4 to 6.

Garnish each serving plate with sliced **fresh jicama,** a few snips of **cilantro** or **parsley** and a sprinkle of **lemon juice.**

*Remember to always keep hands away from the face, especially the eyes.

For the above recipe use Chimayo or New Mexico chiles, grown in New Mexico, or Anaheim or California chiles, grown in California.

Three Men Bearing Gifts

This bowl is painted with an unmarried girl at center and three men offering gifts. The man with the parrot is wearing a belt and headdress that is often seen in association with performing parrots. One man is offering a rabbit and another is offering a fish.

For eons The People have gathered the fruits and seeds that Mother Earth naturally provides. As the wild berries ripen the Pueblo peoples collect the tiny tasty fruits as fast as they can, before the birds and bears eat them all!

Berries & Cream

1 1/2 cups fresh blueberries
1 1/2 cups fresh blackberries
1 1/2 cups fresh raspberries
3/4 cups sugar
4 T. rum or 1 t. rum extract
1/2 pint whipping cream

Frozen berries may be used for this recipe. Keep the berries frozen until you are ready to use them. Rinse fresh berries in cold running water in a strainer and drain.

In a small saucepan over low heat, combine sugar and rum, stirring constantly until sugar is dissolved. Cool for 10 minutes. Pour over berries. Refrigerate until ready to use. Spoon berries into individual serving bowls. Top with cream, whipped or plain. Serves 4 to 6.

Bow Hunter with Slain Deer

This hunter has been successful and has slain a deer to feed the people. The body of the deer now displays the diamond pattern (or square) representing the "center" or pueblo where the people live. The hunter holds a prayer stick above the deer with one hand and his other hand is touching the deer. He is praying and thanking the animal directly for its sacrifice. If he performs all of these prayers well the animal will reincarnate and sacrifice itself again to feed The People another day.

When the Spaniards marched north from Mexico and into the Southwest they searched for the Seven Cities of Gold. A thousand men under the command of Coronado streamed through the mountains and brought with them herds of sheep and cattle. While these animals had never before been seen in the west, they quickly became an integral part of the diet and culture of the Indians, Spanish and Anglo pioneers.

Simmering Beef Pot

2 1/2 pounds lean chuck, cut into 1-inch cubes
3 cups beef broth or water
2 slices bacon, cut into small pieces
2 T. olive or vegetable oil
3 T. all-purpose or enriched white flour
1 large onion, coarsely chopped
1 clove garlic, diced
1 fresh green chile pepper, seeded and chopped or
      1 can (4 oz.) diced green chiles, drained
1 jalapeño chile pepper, seeded and diced
1 t. salt
1/2 t. freshly ground black pepper
3/4 t. oregano
1/4 t. cumin
2 cups canned garbanzo beans, drained
2 T. sun-dried tomato pieces or 2 fresh tomatoes,
      chopped
1/4 cup fresh cilantro, chopped

In a large pot or dutch oven, cover meat with the beef broth (or water). Bring to a boil, reduce heat, cover and simmer for 1 1/2 hours. In a medium skillet fry the bacon until crisp and reserve. Add oil to skillet. Over medium heat add flour and stir constantly until flour browns. Remove skillet from heat and immediately stir in the onion and garlic. Add to the beef along with the remaining ingredients (except cilantro and bacon). Cover and simmer for an additional hour. Add bacon. Garnish individual bowls of soup with cilantro. Serves 4 to 6.

Man with Burden Basket & Fertility Staff

This may be an illustration of the notorious, mythological, Kokopelli. Legend claims that he traveled to the northern pueblos from the south and brought exotic goods to trade which he carried in his pack. Other stories have him supplying the seeds that the people foolishly forgot during their migration, or ascension, from the underworld up to this, the fourth world. The figure is clearly male, complete with hair cue. He is holding a fertility staff. The end of the staff represents the male genitalia and the cross just below represents the female fertility elements. The zig-zag pattern on the lower staff is also a symbol of fertility. From around A.D. 500 to A.D. 1325 fertility was the basis of Pueblo religious practice.

Attributable to the Navajo, fry bread is one of the most common modern Native foods regardless of tribal affiliations. The basic ingredients suffer the variations inflicted by one chef to another and the dough may be patted out round, square or in triangular shapes, but it is still, unmistakably, fry bread—no matter where or how you find it.

Fry Bread

3 cups all-purpose or enriched white flour
1 T. baking powder
1 t. salt
1 1/2 cups warm water or milk
1 T. vegetable oil
oil or shortening for frying

In a mixing bowl combine all ingredients and knead until smooth. Brush oil over top of dough, cover and allow to rest for 30 minutes. On a lightly floured board, using a lightly floured rolling pin, roll into circles that are approximately 4 inches in diameter and 1/8" thick. Deep fry in the oil or shortening until flecked with brown, turning carefully, once. Drain on paper towels. Makes 10 to 12 breads.

Dragonfly

According to Hopi mythology dragonflies were sent by Oman to reopen springs which Muingwa had destroyed. In Pueblo mythologies the dragonflies are a water symbol and bring rains in times of drought. In the high desert, dragonflies are regarded as the guardians of the springs.

Greens grow wild and can be easily gathered by those who know what to put in their baskets. Purslane, tumbleweed, dandelions, spinach, mustard greens, amaranth and many more delicious leafy plants abound in the Southwest. The early Jesuit Priests reported that the Pueblo Indians were especially fond of amaranth patches.

Fresh Greens & Herb Salad

4 to 6 cups of your choice of the following:

spinach	amaranth*
fresh young sorrel*	red oak leaf
arugula	lettuce
red cabbage, sliced very thin	radicchio
fresh young dandelions*	chervil
red romaine	perilla
fresh young tumbleweed*	frisée

1 cup of all or your choice of the following:

fresh chives	fresh basil
fresh green onions	fresh mint
fresh shallots	fresh cilantro
fresh oregano	fresh parsley

Tear greens into bite-sized pieces. Chop or snip herbs. Combine fresh greens and herbs in a glass bowl. Toss gently and refrigerate until eady to use. Drizzle salad with **Honey Dressing** and garnish with **feta cheese,** a sprinkle of roasted **pine nuts** or **sunflower seeds** (see page 103), and **edible flowers** (see page 105). Serves 4 to 6.

Honey Dressing

4 T. olive oil	1/2 t. fresh ground
2 T. balsamic vinegar	pepper
1/2 t. salt	1 t. honey

Combine dressing ingredients and chill for at least 1 hour.

*Not available in stores, but easily cultivated. See also page 105.

Beetle, Rabbit & Turkey Tail Combination

Strange animal combinations are not uncommon in Mimbres art. Each individual element could represent inherent characteristics of the animals or a phonetic mix of sounds representing something entirely different.

At Zuni Pueblos the coiled strips of pumpkin drying in the sun on the pueblo rooftops are a common sight. Pumpkins and other squash are dried and then reconstituted into many dishes.

Pumpkin Pudding

2 cups milk or half-and-half
1/3 cup white or yellow cornmeal
1/4 cup pure maple syrup or dark molasses
1/2 cup brown sugar, packed
1/4 cup butter
1 t. salt
1/2 t. cinnamon
1/2 t. cloves
1/2 t. allspice
1/8 t. nutmeg
1 cup canned pumpkin
1 egg, beaten

Preheat the oven to 300°. Using the top of a double boiler bring the milk to a boil. Slowly stir in the cornmeal, then place the mixture over the boiling water and cook for fifteen minutes, stirring occasionally. Stir in the maple syrup or molasses and cook an additional five minutes. Remove from heat and mix in all other ingredients. Pour into a well greased baking dish and bake for 1 1/2 hours. Serve warm with *Sweetened Whipping Cream.* Serves 4 to 6.

Sweetened Whipping Cream

1/2 pint whipping cream
1/4 cup light brown sugar, sifted
1/2 cup pecans, chopped fine

Heat the cream in a small saucepan over medium heat. As the cream is heating slowly add the brown sugar. Stir constantly until sugar is dissolved.

Spoon pudding into small bowls. Spoon cream over the pudding. Sprinkle nuts on top. Pudding may be served warm, at room temperature or chilled.

Fisherman & His Catch

This illustration is reminiscent of the yellowing curling snapshots that you often see in the sporting goods store. The fisherman will be smiling and holding up his or her catch for the camera to document. Here the fisherman is shown with the head of the kingfisher bird. This is probably not a mask. He is such a good fisherman that he is identifying with this expert fishing bird. Notice the fish trap in the background.

Trout from the mountain rivers were speared or captured in woven fish traps. The prehistoric Indians also used walnut hulls (which contain natural toxins) to poison the water and temporarily stun the fish for easy capture.

Trout

4 medium-sized fresh trout
1/2 pound butter
Salt and freshly ground black pepper
3/4 cup light cream
1/2 t. lemon zest
1/4 t. dill weed

Wash the fish and pat them dry. Leave the head and the tail on. Generously salt and pepper inside and out. In a heavy frying pan (choose a pan just large enough to accommodate all of the fish) with a tight fitting lid, melt the butter over medium heat. Turn heat to medium high or high and place the trout in the skillet side by side. Cover and cook for 5 minutes. Turn the fish over and cook for 5 minutes more. Remove from heat. Make a careful cut along the backbone and then gently lift the head of the trout. The bones should follow. Place the trout on a platter to keep warm. The skin of the trout will be very crisp and edible.

Add the cream, lemon zest and dill to the pan juices and simmer until heated through. To serve, spoon the sauce onto each plate, lay the trout on top of the sauce and garnish if desired with sprigs of dill weed.

Note: The success of this dish depends on the use of **very** high heat while frying. Don't be timid. Serves 4.

Serving suggestion: Serve with **Hot Pepper Relish** (see page 101).

Five Corn Maidens

In Mimbres art, very young people are painted with large
heads. These five young girls wear the grid dot and water
symbol headbands of the Corn Maidens. The Corn Maidens are
spirits who return to the pueblo and ensure the corn crop. If
they are insulted or otherwise angered they will leave and
never return and the corn will not ripen.

In the fall, long strings of chiles turn from green to red and from red to black-burgundy as they dry in the Southwestern sun. Ears of corn with husks tied tight add to the dazzling display of color.

Green Chile Corn Bread

4 slices bacon, cut into small pieces
1/2 cup diced onion
1/2 cup diced red bell pepper
1/4 cup all-purpose or enriched white flour
2 cups yellow cornmeal
1 t. salt
2 t. baking powder
1/2 t. baking soda
1 T. sugar
1 cup buttermilk
2 eggs, beaten
1/2 cup cooked corn, drained
1 can (4 oz.) diced green chiles, drained
1 cup grated mild cheddar cheese

Fry bacon until crisp, crumble and set aside. Sauté onions and bell pepper in bacon drippings for two minutes. Set aside. Preheat oven to 350°. Combine flour, cornmeal, salt, baking powder, baking soda and sugar in a large mixing bowl. Add buttermilk and eggs and stir until well-blended. Add onion, bell pepper (including drippings), corn, green chiles and bacon, mixing thoroughly. Grease a 10-inch cast iron skillet. Pour half of the mixture into skillet and sprinkle with half of the cheese. Spoon on the remaining mixture and top with cheese. Bake at 350° for 35 minutes, or until top is golden brown and toothpick inserted into center comes out clean. Serves 4 to 6.

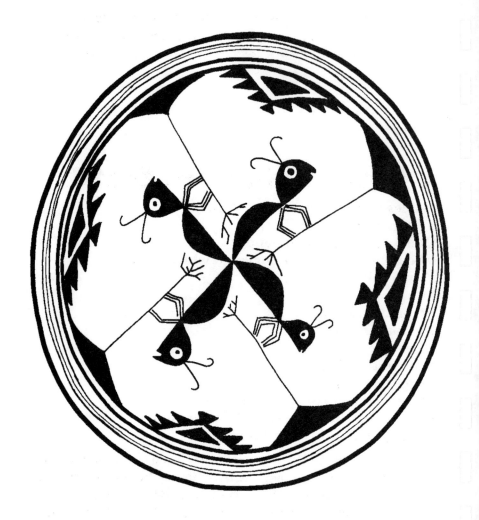

Four Ants on Dead Branches

Insects were one of the more commonly illustrated images of the Mimbres artist. The quadrant layout of the bowl represents the fourth world, the world of the living. Four is the magic number in Mimbres art. The dead sticks or branches upon which the ants perch are uncommon. Plants were rarely represented by the Mimbres.

Hiking in the mountains with my Zuni guide, I became fatigued. As we sat under a bush and enjoyed the shade he offered me a handful of squaw berries and greens he had gathered. "Eat these and you will be refreshed," he said. Perhaps it was the power of suggestion, but I did feel much stronger as we continued our hike. — James

Steamed Greens with Leeks

2 T. butter
4 T. olive oil
1 clove garlic, minced
1 leek, sliced thin, white
    portion only

1 pound spinach
1/2 pound mustard greens
1 cup sorrel or kale
1/2 cup arugula

Heat oil in a large saucepan. Add the garlic and leek and sauté 2 minutes. Wash greens well and remove the stems. Shake off excess water. Add the greens to the leeks, cover and cook over high heat until steam appears. Reduce heat and simmer until tender, about 5 minutes. Serves 4 to 6.*

The following young tender wild greens (see also page 105) may be added if you're lucky enough to find them. Decrease the amount of the last four ingredients above accordingly.

lamb's quarters (lettuce)	shepherd's purse	chickory
purslane	Indian lettuce	burnet
miner's lettuce	spidercoat	borage
	amaranth	dandelion

Sunflower Seed Dressing

2 T. balsamic vinegar
1 t. salt
1/2 t. freshly ground pepper
1/8 t. garlic powder
2 T. raw, hulled sunflower seeds

Combine all ingredients except sunflower seeds and drizzle over each serving of greens. Sprinkle top with sunflower seeds.

* Cooked greens reduce by one-half their original volume.

Two Butterflies with Intertwined Tongues

This use of the insect tongue to represent the spiral is a very common theme in Mimbres art. The spiral usually represents motion, vortex, transcendence or the life breath of the living.

The old orchard at the ranch was so overgrown with weeds and suckers that it took years to cut back. Hacking my way into the thick growth I came upon the huge trunk of an apple tree that had been planted over 100 years ago. The two main trunks of the great tree had suffered an injury. The resident wheelwright had forged a chain of many handmade links and joined the great trunks together. The chain is still there, grown deep into the trunk, a bizarre meld of wood and iron. — James

Baked Apricots & Pears

6 fresh ripe pears, peeled
6 fresh ripe apricots, peeled
1 cup dry red wine
1 cup brown sugar, packed
1 t. allspice
1/8 t. salt
1 lime, seeded and quartered
4 oz. cream cheese, softened
1/2 cup powdered sugar
1/2 cup chopped pecans, walnuts or almonds
whole fresh mint leaves

Preheat oven to 350°. To facilitate peeling fruit, bring water to a boil in a 2-quart saucepan. Remove from heat and carefully place fruit in water. Allow fruit to sit in hot water for 2 minutes. Remove and place in cold water. Peel, halve and pit. Place fruit cut-side up in a baking dish. In a small saucepan, combine and heat, but do not boil, the next five ingredients. Stir, then pour over fruit. Cover baking dish and bake until fork tender, approximately 15 minutes. Discard lime quarters. Cool. Stir together cream cheese and sugar. Place two pear and two apricot halves into individual glass serving dishes. Spoon juice over fruit. Fill centers with cream cheese mixture, sprinkle nuts over tops and garnish each dish with mint leaves. Serves 4 to 6.

Abstract Bowl with Star/Planet Symbols

This abstract bowl is painted with several crosses symbolizing
bright stars or planets. Also depicted are two turkey tails and
an insect. Most Mimbres ceremics are decorated with abstract
rather than figurative designs.

Hominy is traditionally made by soaking dry corn in a mixture of wood or corn cob ashes, powdered lime and water. The thick outer hull and germ are then removed. This posole recipe makes a hearty stew even without the addition of meat.

Pork Posole

2 1/2 pounds lean pork, cut into 1-inch cubes
1 t. salt
1/2 t. freshly ground pepper
4 T. all-purpose or enriched white flour
3 T. olive or vegetable oil
1 large onion, coarsely chopped
1 clove garlic, minced
1/4 t. ground cumin
1 small bay leaf
2 T. sun-dried tomato pieces, or 1 large tomato,
    coarsely chopped
1 large green chile pepper, seeded, coarsely chopped,
    or 1 can (4 oz.) diced green chiles
2 cups canned hominy, drained (or cooked from
    dry hominy)
4 cups water or chicken broth
1/4 cup fresh cilantro, chopped

Mix salt, pepper and flour together. Coat meat with mixture. In a large saucepan or dutch oven heat oil and fry half the meat, onion and garlic until browned. Remove and add second batch of meat, onion and garlic. Brown this batch, then combine the two. Next add all remaining ingredients. Cover, reduce heat and simmer for 30 to 40 minutes, stirring occasionally. Remove bay leaf before serving. Garnish with fresh cilantro. Serves 4 to 6.

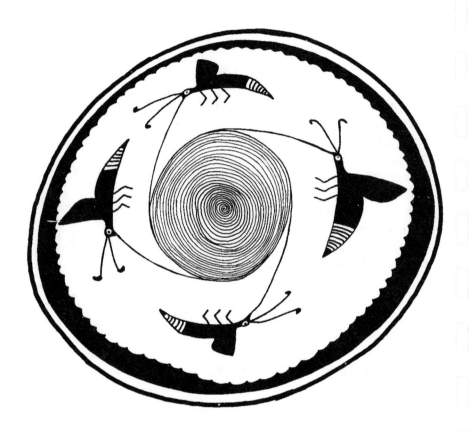

Four Butterflies & Spiral Tongues

Butterflies are female symbols and are associated with fertility. The flitting flight of the butterfly is said to be like the flight of the spirits when they return to visit. The spiral pattern usually indicates motion, transcendence, life breath or life wind.

The dried mesquite bean pod holds a treasure of flavor and nutrients. Ground and added to the flour of breads this unique spice comes alive.

Adobe Bread

1 pkg. (1/4 oz.) active dry yeast
1/4 cup warm water
1 1/2 cups hot water
3 T. lard or vegetable shortening
2 T. honey
1/4 cup mesquite meal
1/4 cup wheat flour
4 cups all-purpose or enriched white flour
1 t. salt
2 T. vegetable oil
2 T. mesquite meal

In a small bowl dissolve the yeast into 1/4 cup of warm water. Set aside. In a small saucepan place 1 1/2 cups of water, shortening and honey. Heat until shortening is melted. Cool to lukewarm. Place honey mixture in a large mixing bowl and stir in dissolved yeast. Sift together the 1/4 cup mesquite meal, flours and salt. Add 1 cup of the flour mixture to the honey mixture. Beat well. Gradually stir in the remaining flour a little at a time, beating well after each addition. The final cup will have to be kneaded in. Knead for ten minutes on a lightly floured surface. Dough should be smooth, stiff, but pliable.

Place dough back in bowl and brush with 1 tablespoon oil. Cover with a cloth and allow to rise in a draft-free place until dough doubles in bulk, usually about one hour. Punch down the dough on a lightly floured surface and knead again for five minutes. Divide the dough in half and place in 2 greased baking bowls, or shape into 2 round loaves and place on a greased baking sheet. Brush tops with remaining oil and sprinkle each with one tablespoon of mesquite meal. Bake for 40 to 50 minutes or until the tops are lightly browned and loaves sound hollow when tapped.

This recipe works well with bread machines. Follow manufacturer's directions.

Spider Grandmother

Spider Grandmother is the embodiment of Mother Earth. She is the one who helps the Warrior Twins while they are on their adventures. She feeds them and gives them special weapons and prayers. All mythologies throughout the world have a Spider Grandmother. The recent Star Wars Trilogy included two; Obi-wan and Yoda.

I hike along the prehistoric irrigation ditches of the Upper Little Colorado River and collect the wild grapes, mint leaves and watercress that cling to life along this tiny riparian environment. Only two feet wide but many miles long, the damp banks that were dug with digging sticks centuries ago provide the habitat for a cornucopia of fragile life. — James

Cucumbers & Watercress Salad

1 medium cucumber, unpeeled
1 small bunch watercress (approximately 1 cup)
2 green onions, thinly sliced diagonally

Wash and then score the cucumber lengthwise with the tines of a fork. Slice cucumber widthwise into very thin slices. In individual glass bowls, arrange slices over the watercress. Top with the green onions and drizzle with **Lemon Juice Dressing.** Chill before serving. Serves 4 to 6.

Lemon Juice Dressing

3 T. olive oil
2 T. lemon juice
1/2 t. salt
1/4 t. freshly ground black pepper
1 t. fresh dill weed, snipped (or 1/4 t. dried)

Mix together well and chill.

Honey Gatherer & Butterflies

Butterflies were almost always shown with the white dots on the margins of their wings. Here they steal a sip of honey from the Honey Gatherer.

When we moved to the old ranch the derelict bunkhouse was home to several hives of wild bees. After several exciting days of honey harvesting with the help of a local beekeeper we stood back and admired twenty gallons of the golden amber. — James

Honeyed Applesauce

4 cups dried apple chunks
4 cups water
3/4 t. vanilla
3 T. honey
3 T. mesquite meal

In a medium saucepan cover the apples with water. Cover the pan, bring to a boil, and reduce heat. Cook for 2 minutes. Remove from the heat and, still covered, allow to rest for about 2 hours. Resume cooking over medium heat until soft (approximately 30 minutes). Add the vanilla and honey. Cook two more minutes. Portion into individual bowls, sprinkle 1/2 tablespoon of mesquite meal on top. Serves 4 to 6.

Note: Dried apples retain a firmer consistency than fresh apples and will not fall apart when cooked.

Two Quail & Hatching Eggs

Quail were trapped in nets and represented an important food source for the Mimbres Indians. The checkerboard pattern is shown in association with the quail. This pattern is very commonly illustrated with animals on the bowls that were buried with the dead. The checkerboard represents the Milky Way or pathway of the Warrior Twins, Brother Elder and Brother Younger.

Coveys of quail run across the desert with their top notches bobbing and their chicks chasing behind. These delicate birds were netted by the prehistoric Pueblo Indians in community game drives.

Roasted Game Birds with White Currant Stuffing

**6 game birds such as quail or dove, or Rock
   Cornish hens
2 T. butter, melted**

Preheat oven to 500° and prepare **White Currant Stuffing** (See page 71). Clean cavities of birds, reserving giblets, and rinse thoroughly under cool water. Pat birds dry, then salt inside and out.

Stuff body of birds loosely. Close neck flap with a skewer. Cover any exposed stuffing with foil to prevent drying. Wing tips should be tucked under bird and tied in place.

Brush birds with melted butter and salt lightly. Reduce oven heat to 350°. Place birds breast side up on a rack in a shallow baking pan and put into oven. Baste several times with pan juices. Roast approximately one hour or until birds are nicely browned and juices run clear. Do not overcook. After roasting is completed, remove birds to a platter and keep warm. Serves 4 to 6.

Gravy

**2 cups chicken broth
2 T. cornstarch
2 T. water**

Add broth to roasting pan juices and deglaze. Combine cornstarch and water and slowly stir into simmering broth. Cook for two minutes, stirring constantly.

(Continued on page 71)

Lizards

Lizards were abundantly illustrated by the Mimbres painters.
Images of lizards also abound in the petroglyphic images of the
Southwest. The lizard likeness is a reflection of the Pueblo
Creation myth: *When The People lived below in the third world
they had tails, webbed digits and genitals on top of their heads.
They crawled up through the sipapu and became human with
the help of the Warrior Twins.*

Sunflower seeds were primarily winnowed, dried, ground on metates and eaten as a mush. Sunflowers were semi-domesticated even before corn and beans. Hopi girls still grind the petals of the sunflower and mix them with cornmeal for use as a ceremonial powder.

(Continued from page 69)

White Currant Stuffing

2 T. butter
2 green onions, sliced thin (use entire onion)
reserved giblets, chopped fine
3 cups day-old bread broken into 1/2-inch cubes
1/4 cup dried white currants
2 T. raw, hulled sunflower seeds
3/4 t. salt
1/2 t. white pepper
1/2 t. sage, dried or 2 T. fresh, chopped
1 T. fresh parsley, chopped
1 egg
2 T. water

Heat butter in large skillet. Add onion and giblets and sauté for two minutes. Add remaining ingredients and mix well.

Rabbit/Rattlesnake Combination

Animal combinations were very frequently created by the Mimbres artist. These undoubtedly have specific mythological significance. Snakes are the guardians of underground water sources and represent renewal because they shed their skins and are reborn. Rabbits are fertility symbols and are associated with the moon which is reborn each month.

Squash has been an important part of the Native American diet for thousands of years. The Zuni dry the squash in spiral strips on their pueblo rooftops. In a cool, dry environment squash will keep for more than a year, well into the next harvest.

Squash, Minted Peas & Baby Pearl Onions

2 butternut or acorn squash, unpeeled
2 cups peas, fresh or frozen
1 T. butter
1 T. fresh mint, minced
1/2 cup baby pearl onions, from a jar

Preheat oven to 350°. Wash and slice the squash lengthwise. Remove seeds and membranes and place each half in a baking dish, cut side down. Add 1" of water and bake for about an hour, depending upon squash size. Meanwhile cook the peas in lightly salted water. Drain. Add the butter, mint and onions. To serve, place squash on serving plates and spoon pea mixture into the center of squash. Serves 4.

Long-Tailed Cat

Mountain lions were usually illustrated by the Mimbres artist with very long, exaggerated tails. This treatment is similar to the embellishment seen with the necks of cranes and the tails of turkeys. Mountain lions are associated with the color yellow and the direction North in Pueblo mythologies.

The Spanish priests planted peach trees near their missions. This fruit became a favorite among the Hopi who dried them and used the peaches for trade with their Navajo neighbors.

Peach Crisp

6 large ripe peaches
1/4 cup honey
1 t. ginger, freshly grated
3/4 cup all-purpose or enriched white flour
1/4 cup mesquite meal
3/4 cup brown sugar, packed
1/2 cup cold butter
1/2 cup pecans, finely chopped

Preheat oven to 375°. Make a small cross-slit on stem end of peaches and place in boiling water for about 2 minutes. Rinse peaches under cold water. Skin, pit and slice. Place peach slices in a 2-quart baking dish. Drizzle honey over the top. Add grated ginger and toss. In a small bowl, combine the flour, mesquite meal and brown sugar. Cut in butter until the mixture is crumbly. Sprinkle flour mixture evenly over the peaches. Sprinkle the top with nuts. Bake until bubbly and brown, about 30 minutes. Serves 4 to 6.

Man Spearing Fish

This image has been interpreted by some researchers to represent a Mimbreno fisherman encountering a whale. Trading expeditions to the Sea of Cortez and even to the Pacific Ocean did occur and an encounter with a beached whale may have actually happened. Or, a more likely scenario is that this is an exaggeration by a boastful fisherman.

Stories of fish abound in Pueblo mythologies. In one legend The People were on a migration. They came to the shore of a huge lake and waded in, trying to cross. They began to drown. The Warrior Twins arrived and turned the people into fish so they could safely swim across the lake. Once on the other side the Twins turned them back into people.

Cornmeal Coated Catfish

2 cups yellow cornmeal
2 T. all-purpose or enriched white flour
1 t. salt
1/2 t. cayenne pepper
1/4 t. cumin
2 pounds catfish fillets
2 egg whites, stiffly beaten
1/2 cup vegetable oil
lemon wedges
young, thin, whole green onions

Combine all of the dry ingredients. Rinse fish thoroughly and pat dry. Dip the fish in the egg whites and then coat well with the dry ingredients. In a large skillet over medium-high heat, heat the oil and fry the fillets for about 5 minutes per side or until they are golden brown and flake easily. (Cook's rule of thumb: fish take approximately 10 minutes per inch of thickness to cook through.) Drain on paper towels. Garnish with lemon wedges and green onions. Serves 4.

Men Gardening

The Mimbres artists often illustrated day-to-day activities. These illustrations are some of the best evidence that remains of their lifeways. These men are working the garden using digging sticks. The figures are identified as men by the presence of their hair cues and genitalia. The plants are probably a bean crop and are clearly planted in rows. Notice the cat in the illustration. There is no archaeological evidence that the Pueblo Indians raised domestic cats. However, they were a frequent inclusion in Mimbres paintings and are usually shown in domestic scenes.

Today, Anasazi beans are commercially grown in only one region of Colorado. Over 1500 years ago beans were introduced into the Southwest from Mexico. Pottery may have evolved in order to soak and cook the beans.

Anasazi Beans

2 cups Anasazi Beans®, uncooked
1 medium onion, chopped
1 clove garlic, minced
1/2 cup thin sliced celery
1 t. salt
1 1/2 t. freshly ground black pepper
1 t. pure chile powder, mild
1 pinch chipotle pepper or 1 jalepeño pepper,
seeded and diced
1/4 t. ground cumin
1/2 t. Mexican oregano
1/4 t. thyme
1/4 t. basil
1/2 t. grated lemon peel
2 T. sun-dried tomato pieces or 1 large tomato,
coarsley chopped
1 bay leaf

Clean and sort beans. Cover with water and soak for approximately 12 hours. Fast method: bring beans to a boil for 2 minutes, cover, and allow to rest for one hour.

Drain beans and add 4 cups of water. Cover, bring to a boil, reduce heat and simmer for 1 to 1 1/2 hours or until nearly tender. Add all other ingredients (except salt*) and cook, uncovered, for approximately 1 hour or to desired consistency. Check liquid level from time to time, adding more water if necessary. Serve with warmed corn or flour tortillas. Serves 4.

*Cook's rule of thumb: When cooking dried beans, never add salt until beans are nearly tender. Adding salt too early prevents beans from softening. Also, remember to remove the bay leaf before serving.

Man in Prayer

This raised-arm stance is one of the most common petroglyphic symbols found throughout the greater Southwest. The man is praying to the gods with his arms and hands raised to the heavens. The grid dot pattern on his body represents corn.

Citrus fruits were brought from Europe to the Americas in the early part of the 16th century by the Spaniards. They carried the fruit aboard ship, eating it to prevent scurvy.

Citrus Salad

curly endive
3 oranges
3 grapefruit
2 T. honey
1/4 t. lime zest
1/8 t. diced fresh ginger
1 T. chopped fresh mint

Wash the endive, tear into bite-sized pieces and arrange on individual plates. Peel fruit and remove the membranes. Break fruit into segments and arrange on top of the greens. In a small saucepan combine the honey, lime zest and ginger. Cook for about 2 minutes stirring constantly. Remove from the heat and cool for 10 minutes. Drizzle over the fruit. Garnish with fresh mint. Serves 4 to 6.

Turtle with Checkerboard Shell

The turtle represents ancestors and longevity. The Zuni Indians perform a pilgrimage once a year walking from their northwestern New Mexico pueblo, over sixty miles south, to collect turtles. These they worship as their ancestors. The checkerboard pattern on the shell of the turtle represents the Milky Way which was a pathway for the Warrior Twins. Notice the square spiral patterning within the border of the bowl. This is the symbol for a turtle.

At the ranch, there is an old pear tree. Just a broken stump with a rotted and aging center of soft and fragile wood. It has been repaired many times with iron and concrete props, like many needed crutches, but still produces a few pears every year, on a single leafy branch. — James

Little Fruit-filled Pies

2 cups all-purpose or
   enriched white flour
1 t. salt
1/4 cup sugar
1 t. baking powder
2/3 cup vegetable shortening,
   chilled

2 T. butter, chilled
4 to 5 T. cold water
1 egg yolk
1 T. milk
1/4 cup powdered
   sugar

Preheat oven to 425°. Sift together flour, salt, sugar and baking powder. Work in half of the shortening and the butter with fingertips until dough resembles the texture of cornmeal. Add remaining shortening and butter and work in until dough is pea-sized. Sprinkle with water, mixing with a fork *only until it can be gathered into a ball.* On a lightly floured board, roll dough to 1/8 inch thick. Cut into squares. Moisten edges with water. Place 1 tablespoonful **Fruit Filling** in center. Fold over into a triangle. Crimp edges with a fork. Make one small slit on top. Brush tops with egg yolk and milk which have been beaten together. Bake on ungreased cookie sheet until golden brown (approximately 15 minutes). Sift powdered sugar over warm pies. Makes 14 pies.

Fruit Filling

1 cup uncooked dried apricots,
   peaches or pears, or a
   combination
1 1/4 cups water

1/4 t. cinnamon
1/8 t. ginger
2/3 cup sugar

Bring fruit and water to a boil in medium-sized saucepan. Remove from heat, cover and allow to rest for 1/2 hour. Cook again over medium heat until fruit is soft, approximately 30 minutes. Remove from heat and mash with a fork. Add sugar and spices and continue cooking over low heat for 10 more minutes.

Rabbit & Fertility Staff

Rabbits represent the moon and fertility. The arch of the rabbit's body resembles the crescent moon. In the full moon the rabbit can be seen dancing on the surface. The fertility staff includes the elements that represent man and woman. The zig-zag pattern on the staff is also a symbol for fertility.

Prehistorically, rabbits were hunted by stretching nets across the bottoms of canyons. Rabbits and other small game were driven into the nets and then killed with throwing sticks. These rabbit throwing sticks resemble the boomerang of the Australian Aborigines.

Braised Rabbit with White Beans

1 rabbit, approximately 4 pounds
1 1/2 T. olive or vegetable oil
1 1/2 T. butter
1 medium onion, chopped
1 clove garlic, minced
1 1/2 t. salt
1 t. freshly ground pepper
1 cup chopped celery, (include leaves)
1/2 cup chopped carrots
1 bay leaf
5 cups chicken broth or water
3 cups Great Northern white beans, canned or cooked
1 large tomato, chopped
1/4 cup tarragon vinegar
2 T. fresh parsley, chopped
4 T. cornstarch
8 T. water
2 green onions, greens and all, thinly sliced

Skin, clean and section the rabbit. In a large Dutch oven, heat the oil and butter over medium heat, add the rabbit and brown on one side. Turn rabbit, add onion and garlic and continue browning. Add salt, pepper, celery, carrots, bay leaf and broth. Cover, reduce heat and simmer for 30 minutes. Add drained beans, tomato and vinegar. Cover and simmer an additional 30 minutes. Remove the bay leaf. Add parsley. Mix cornstarch with water and slowly stir into broth. Simmer five more minutes stirring occasionally. Serve, garnished with green onions over a bed of *Rice, Wild and Brown!* (see page 87.) Serves 4 to 6.

Mother Skunk & Four Babies

Four is the magic number in Mimbres mythology. The fourth
world of existence is the world of the living. The number four
is the most repeated numerical element in Mimbres art. This
mother skunk holds a bee in her mouth.

Wild rice is best known for its use by the Indians of the Great Lakes Region. The Algonquian tribes harvested this abundant staple for centuries and the grains were widely traded.

Rice, Wild & Brown!

1 cup brown rice (basmati is best)
1/2 cup wild rice

Soak rice in HOT water for 25 minutes. Drain well.

3 T. olive oil
1/4 cup finely chopped onion
1 clove garlic, minced
1 t. salt
1/2 t. freshly ground pepper
1/4 t. tumeric
3 cups beef broth
2 T. cilantro, chopped

Heat the oil in a heavy saucepan. Add the brown rice, wild rice, onion and garlic and cover with a tight fitting lid. Cook over medium-high heat until rice is opaque. Add beef broth, bring mixture to a boil and continue boiling for 2 minutes. Cover saucepan, reduce heat to low and simmer for 40 minutes (do not lift lid). Remove pan from heat, fluff rice with a fork, stir in cilantro and replace lid. Allow mixture to rest for about 10 minutes before serving. Serves 4 to 6.

Ladybug with Checkerboard Back

Many insects and insect combinations are shown in Mimbres art. This ladybug is adorned with the checkerboard pattern which indicates the Milky Way or "starry sky". Many night images are depicted in the art of the Mimbrenos. This may be due to the use of these bowls as grave goods and because the night was associated with the dead.

The Aztec Indians in MesoAmerica enjoyed guacamole thousands of years ago. Back then it was made with tomatoes, avocados, chiles and agave worms!

Tomato Avocado Salad

fresh green lettuce leaves
3 ripe avocados
3 ripe tomatoes
3 green onions, sliced thin diagonally
2 T. chopped fresh cilantro

Tear lettuce leaves into bite-sized pieces and place on individual glass plates. Cut avocados and tomatoes into wedges and arrange over lettuce. Garnish with onions and cilantro. Drizzle *Lime Dressing* over salad. Serve immediately. Serves 4 to 6.

Lime Dressing

6 T. olive or vegetable oil
1 T. fresh lime juice
1 T. rice vinegar
1/4 t. salt
1/8 t. freshly ground black pepper
pinch of sugar

Combine and beat with a wire whisk. Chill.

Serving suggestion: Garnish with **chive blossoms.**

Lady & Performing Parrots

Her long elegant sash and fancy sandals indicate a costume. She wears a parrot mask and holds a small staff indicating authority. One parrot performs in a hoop while another waits in a crate. Live parrots were brought from central America and traded throughout the Southwest. They were valued for their colorful feathers and ability to mimic human speech and song.

With the exception of wild honey, the Pueblo Indians had few sweeteners. To create a mixture that was used as a general sweetener, young girls were chosen to chew new corn kernels which, when mixed with their saliva, turned the starch of the corn into a sugar.

Pueblo Bread Pudding

4 cups toasted or stale bread
3 cups warm milk
1/4 t. salt
3 egg yolks
1/2 cup brown sugar, packed
1/2 t. cinnamon
1/4 cup raisins or currants
1/2 cup grated sharp cheddar cheese
1/4 cup maple syrup

Preheat oven to 350°. Remove crusts and break bread into 1" pieces. Soak the bread for 15 minutes in warm milk to which salt has been added. Combine egg yolks with brown sugar, beat well and add the next three ingredients. Add to the soaked bread mixture and mix lightly with a fork. Pour into buttered 2-quart baking dish. Set baking dish in a baking pan of hot water. Bake approximately 30 minutes. Remove from oven and drizzle maple syrup over the top. Bake for another 15 minutes or until knife inserted near middle comes out clean. Serve warm with **Spiced Cream Sauce** or **Jam Sauce** spooned over top. Serves 4 to 6.

Spiced Cream Sauce

1 cup powdered sugar
1/2 t. cinnamon
1/4 t. cloves
1/8 t. salt
1/2 cup heavy cream
1 t. rum

Combine first four ingredients. Gradually stir in cream (at room temperature) until mixture is the consistency of thin icing.

Jam Sauce

1/2 cup elderberry, currant, raspberry, peach
   or tart cherry jam or preserves
1 cup water
1/4 t. almond extract

Combine jam (or preserves) and water in a small saucepan. Boil for 2 minutes. Remove from heat and stir in extract.

Two Ducks

Ducks were messengers in Pueblo mythologies. They gave
warnings and told when spring was coming. The wavy lines
between the two ducks symbolize song, voice or communication.

Indians listen to the ducks, who signal the arrival of spring and warn of the coming of winter. Ducks sit quietly on the pond until they are disturbed and then rocket into the air in a ruckus of quacks and squawks and a rain of downy feathers.

Roasted Duck with Cornmeal-Pine Nut Stuffing

2 (four to five lb.) ducklings

Preheat oven to 500°. To prepare the ducks, clean the cavities and rinse thoroughly with cool water. Pat the outsides dry. Salt birds inside and out. Stuff loosely with *Cornmeal-Pine Nut Stuffing* and secure the neck flap with skewers. Cover any exposed stuffing with foil to prevent dryness. Pierce the skin repeatedly with a fork to allow excess grease to escape. Place ducks on a rack, breast side up, in oven and immediately reduce heat to 350°. Several times during the roasting process, baste the ducks and then remove the excess grease with baster. Allow 20 minutes baking time per pound. Roast until skin is crisp and juices run clear. Remove ducks to a platter and keep warm. Serves 8 to 12. For gravy, see *Roasted Game Birds* (page 69).

Cornmeal-Pine Nut Stuffing

2 T. vegetable oil
4 T. chopped onion
4 T. thinly sliced celery
2 cups day-old bread,
    broken into 1/2" cubes
2 cups day-old cornbread,
    crumbled
1 t. salt

1 t. freshly ground black
    pepper
1/2 t. thyme
3 T. raw pine nuts
2 T. chopped fresh
    cilantro
2 eggs
1/4 cup chicken broth

Heat oil in a large skillet and sauté the onion and celery for 2 minutes. Add the next 9 ingredients and mix well.

The Warrior Twins Recovering the Clouds

The Warrior Twins, Brother Elder and Brother Younger, are two mischievous brothers who fill the Pueblo stories with laughter and grand adventure. Here they are shown retrieving the clouds from the belly of the Cloud Swallower Monster. The monster had swallowed all of the clouds and there was no rain. With the help of a special rope provided by Spider Grandmother they recover the clouds, the rain, and the crops for the people.

Corn in the Southwest requires many prayers. The Zuni Corn Priest plants a feathered prayer stick in the center of the field and prays that the clouds will cover the crop with sweet rain.

Corn & Peppers

2 slices bacon cut small
4 T. finely chopped green bell pepper
4 T. finely chopped red bell pepper
1/2 t. salt
1/2 t. pepper
1/2 t. pure chile powder, mild
1 t. finely chopped fresh parsley
2 cups fresh or frozen corn, cooked and drained
1 cup canned white hominy, (or, cooked dry hominy)

In a small skillet, render the fat from the bacon. Reserve the bacon. Stir-fry the peppers for 2 minutes in the bacon fat. Add salt and pepper, chile powder and parsley.

In a medium-sized baking dish combine all ingredients except bacon. Crumble bacon on top of mixture and keep mixture warm in oven until serving time. Serves 4 to 6.

Two Scorpions

Here the Mimbres artist painted two bold illustrations of the scorpion. The diamond pattern on the backs of the arachnids often represents the "center". The center of the swastika, or four directions, is the square or diamond pattern. Scorpions are Underworld figures. They live under rocks and logs and are associated with the world of the dead. Modern traditional Native Americans will not view images of the centipede or scorpion for fear of infection by bad spirit magic from the Underworld.

Squash has been cultivated for centuries in the arid Southwest. The long, green zucchini will out-produce any other variety of squash. One or two plants in the garden will fill your table with a bounty throughout the growing season.

Zucchini Bread

3 cups all-purpose or enriched white flour
1 t. salt
1 t. baking soda
1 cup sugar
1 T. cinnamon
1 t. vanilla
3 eggs
1 cup vegetable oil
1/2 cup sour cream
1 cup chopped walnuts or pecans
2 cups unpeeled grated zucchini

Preheat oven to 350°. Grease and lightly flour two 5 x 9 loaf pans. Mix all ingredients together and pour the mixture into the loaf pans. Bake for 1 hour and 20 minutes or until a toothpick inserted into the middle comes out clean. Makes 2 loaves.

Serving suggestion: Serve with a fruit sorbet.

Salsas & Relishes

There are innumerable varieties of salsas made from chiles and tomatoes, and relishes made from corn and zucchini. Cooked or fresh and flavored to partner alongside simmering stews and hearthbreads, these side dishes are invaluable accompaniments.

Jalapeño Brown Salsa

2 T. olive oil
4 jalapeños, seeded and thinly sliced
1 small white onion, chopped fine
2 cloves garlic, minced
1 cup tamari sauce

Heat oil in a small saucepan. Sauté jalapeños, onions and garlic until tender. Add tamari sauce and simmer uncovered for 15 minutes. Keeps for weeks if refrigerated. Use on meats, rice, pasta and cooked vegetables. Yields 1 3/4 cups.

Fresh Green Chile Salsa

1 clove garlic, mashed to a paste
1 fresh jalapeño pepper, seeded and minced
1 green onion, very thinly sliced, using part
    of the green leaves
4 large fresh green chiles, roasted, peeled,
    seeded and minced (see page 102)
2 large fresh, ripe tomatoes, coarsely chopped
4 T. fresh lime juice
4 T. fresh cilantro, minced
1 T. olive oil
1 t. salt

Mix all ingredients together. Cover and refrigerate at least 4 hours to blend flavors. Will keep (refrigerated) for 2 weeks. Good as a dip, on meat and eggs, or on tacos and quesadillas. Yields 2 1/2 cups.

Green Chile Salsa

4 T. olive oil
1 medium-sized onion, diced
2 cloves garlic, minced
4 T. all-purpose or enriched white flour
1 can (16 oz.) chopped green chiles, drained
1 can (16 oz.) chopped tomatoes, drained
1 1/2 t. Mexican oregano
1/4 t. cumin
1 t. salt
2 cups chicken broth

Heat oil over medium-high heat in a 2-quart saucepan. Sauté onion and garlic until transparent. Stir in flour and cook until slightly browned. Mix in chiles, tomatoes, oregano, cumin and salt. Slowly stir in broth. Cook, stirring occasionally, until thickened. Continue cooking over low heat for an additional 15 minutes. Good over burritos, enchiladas or as the basis for green chile stew. Yields 2-1/2 cups.

Chile Salsa #1

6 ripe plum tomatoes, chopped fine
1 large fresh mild green chile, seeded and diced
2 fresh jalapeños, seeded and diced
3 green onions, diced (stem and all)
1 clove garlic, minced
1/4 c. fresh cilantro, chopped fine
1/2 t. Mexican oregano
2 T. lime juice
1 t. salt (or to taste)

By hand or using a food processor, prepare vegetables. Mix together. Add oregano, lime juice and salt. Refrigerate at least 4 hours before serving. Will keep for 2 weeks refrigerated. Good as a dip, on tacos, burritos, eggs or beans. Yields 4-1/2 cups.

Chile Salsa #2

1/2 medium-sized onion
1 clove garlic
1 can (16 oz.) tomato sauce
1 t. Mexican oregano
1/2 t. cumin
1 t. sugar
2 T. pure chile powder, mild or hot
1 t. salt
2 T. water

In a food processor, purée onion and garlic. Place all ingredients together in a medium-sized saucepan. Simmer (uncovered) for 15 minutes. Serve hot or cold. Good as a dip, over tacos, enchiladas, quesadillas, or eggs. Yields 2 1/2 cups.

Tomatillo Salsa

10 fresh medium-sized tomatillos
5 fresh green chiles, seeded
1 fresh jalapeño, seeded (2 if you dare)
2 green onions, sliced (green leaves and all)
2 cloves garlic, chopped
1 t. salt
1 t. lime zest
2 T. fresh cilantro, chopped
1 cup sour cream (optional)

Bring water to a boil in a large saucepan. Remove papery husks of tomatillos by running under warm water. One by one, drop tomatillos into boiling water. Simmer until slightly softened (approximately 5 minutes). Drain and cool. Purée tomatillos in a food processor, then remove and place in a bowl. Add chiles, jalapeño, onion and garlic to processor and finely chop. Blend together salt, lime zest, cilantro and puréed tomatillos in processor. If using sour cream, blend in just before using. Good on rice, pasta, eggs, and meat. Yields 3 cups.

Fresh Cucumber-Zucchini Relish

A good use for an over-abundant supply of cucumbers and zucchini.

12 large cucumbers
12 medium-sized zucchini
2 large onions
1 large red bell pepper
1 large green bell pepper

1 1/2 qts. water
1/4 c. salt
1 small bunch dill
2 c. sugar
1 c. cider vinegar

Wash vegetables well. In a food processor, dice cucumber, zucchini, onion and peppers in batches. Place in a colander and press out excess liquid. Set aside in a large glass container. Bring water and salt to a boil. Pour over vegetables, add dill. Cover and refrigerate for 12 hours. In a medium-sized saucepan boil sugar and vinegar, stirring, until sugar dissolves. Pour syrup over drained vegetables. Serve fresh (will keep for months refrigerated) or process in jars according to manufacturer's directions. Yields 8 qts.

Hot Pepper Relish

2 ea. fresh green, red
    and yellow bell peppers
4 fresh green chile peppers,
    seeded
2 fresh jalapeño peppers,
    seeded
2 medium-sized onions
1 qt. water

2 T. salt
1/2 t. ground coriander
1 t. allspice
2 bay leaves
1 1/2 cups sugar
1 1/2 cups white wine
    vinegar

Wash vegetables well. In a food processor, dice peppers and onions in batches. Place in a glass container and set aside. Bring water and salt to a boil and pour over vegetables. Add coriander, allspice and bay leaves to mixture. Cover and refrigerate for 12 hours. Remove bay leaves. In a medium-sized saucepan boil sugar and vinegar, stirring until sugar dissolves. Pour syrup over drained vegetables. Serve fresh (will keep for months refrigerated) or process in jars according to manufacturer's directions. Yields 4 qts.

Chiles

These delicious gems range from mild to incendiary, adding zest to all manner of dishes. The "heat" of the chile comes from the chemical compound capsaicin which all chiles contain.

The following chiles are commonly used in southwest cuisine. Some may be obtainable only at specialty stores or by mail order. Based on the Scoville Units, the following peppers are rated on a heat scale from 1-10. Be aware however, that soil conditions, climate, elevation and seasonal effects can change the rating in either direction.

Anaheim (California)	2	Habanero	10
Ancho (smoked, dried poblano)	3	Jalapeño	5
Cayenne	8	New Mexico (Chimayo)	2
Cherry	5	Poblano	3
Chile de Arbol	7	Pasilla	3
Chiltepin (found wild)	9	Pequín	8
Chipotle (smoked, dried jalapeño)	5	Serrano	7

Red chiles are ripened, mature green chiles. Chile powder, not to be confused with "chili powder" (which has been adulterated with, among other spices, oregano and cumin), is pure powder, ground from any number of varieties of chiles.

Roasting Chiles

A note of precaution—Chiles may be very irritating to the skin so use rubber gloves when handling and always keep hands away from eyes and face. Puncture each chile the whole length with the tip of a paring knife. Place chiles close together in a shallow baking pan and broil about 6 inches from the heat. When blistered and browned, turn over, using tongs. Each side should take 3 to 4 minutes. The chiles should be blistered all around, so it may be necessary to turn them again. Immediately place the chiles in a tightly covered container (pan, paper or plastic bag) for 15 minutes. This steaming process allows the skin to be removed easily. Still using rubber gloves and leaving the stem intact, use a sharp knife to slit the chiles from the stem end to the tip along the perforations. Then from the tip to the stem, carefully remove the skin. Remove the seeds and membranes and, if desired, the stem.

Native Seeds & Nuts

Prehistorically, to native cultures, cultivated and wild seeds, nuts and beans were a major part of the daily diet providing nutrients, texture and variety. Supply was always dependent upon variables, with some seasons providing abundance, others a meager harvest. Survival equated to better methods of cultivation, preservation and preparation.

Nuts:

Acorns	Pecans	Black Walnuts
Chestnuts	Pine Nuts	

Seeds:

Flax	Pumpkin seeds
Jojoba seeds	Sunflower seeds

Sprouting seeds:

Alfalfa	Sesame seeds	Mustard seeds
Fenugreek	Sunflower seeds	

To blanch nuts: After shelling, pour boiling water over nuts briefly. Drain. Wrap in towel to steam, then rub with the towel to remove the skin.

To roast seeds and nuts: Place in 300° oven and heat until fragrant (approximately 10 minutes), shaking sheet occasionally. Or, place in a dry skillet and cook over low heat for a few minutes, stirring constantly.

Cooking Dried Beans

Rinse and sort beans. Cover with water for 12 hours. Drain and rinse again. Cover with water. Bring to a boil in covered saucepan and simmer until nearly tender. Add preferred seasonings.

Fast method: Rinse and sort beans. In a saucepan, cover with water and bring to a boil. Cover and allow to rest for one hour. Drain and cover again with water. Simmer until nearly tender and add preferred seasonings.

Herbs, Spices & Other Ingredients

With the advent of trade and the migration of cultures into the southwest, herbs, spices and the not-so-common ingredients listed below became increasingly more accessible to Native Americans. Herbs and spices are now used extensively, adding interest as a garnish, flavor and scent. Some of the ingredients listed were developed by our native cultures while others evolved through contact. In any case the mix has brought outstanding culinary results.

Common ingredients include:

Allspice	Cilantro	Mexican
Achiote	Cinnamon	oregano
Aznafran	Coriander seeds	Mint
Basil	Cumin	Nutmeg
Chervil	Dill	Savory
Chile powders	Epazote	Tarragon
& flakes	Ginger	Thyme

Most herbs and spices typically used in contemporary Native American cuisine are commonly found in supermarkets, or, in some cases, must be obtained from specialty stores or by mail order. They are meant to accent and enhance the flavors of foods, not to dominate or overwhelm them. Some, but not all, may be used in their fresh form. Dried herbs are much more pungent, so use sparingly. Cook's rule of thumb: 1/4 teaspoon dried, powdered herb equals 3/4 to 1 teaspoon dried, loosely cut herb, which translates to 1-1/2 to 2 teaspoons chopped fresh herb.

Not-so common ingredients include:

Amaranth flour	Hominy	Pinole
Anasazi Beans®	Jicama	Prickly pear fruit
Atole	Juniper berries	Quinoa
Blue cornmeal	Masa harina	Squash blossoms
Cactus pads	Mesquite meal	Tepary beans
Chayote	Parched corn	Tomatillos
Corn husks	Piki bread	Zuni Gold beans
Culinary ash		

Edible Flowers

It's time to give edible flowers their culinary due. All may be used as a garnish, but you'll have to experiment with these fragile beauties to discover their best use. Whether to cook, float, sprinkle, snip, infuse, scent, or to crystallize ... allow your imagination to explore the many possibilities.

Harvest your blossoms, if possible, in the early morning. Gently rinse under cool water and gently pat dry. When ready to use, refresh in ice water and again pat dry. For salads, add blossoms at the last moment after tossing with dressing.

Edible Blossoms & Petals

Almond	English primrose	Pansy
Alyssum	Forget-me-not	Peach
Apple	Fuchsia	Plum
Bee balm	Geranium	Portulaca
Bergamot	Hollyhock	Pot marigold
Borage	Indian	Prickly pear
Calendula	paintbrush	Rose
Chive	Lavender	Rosemary
Chrysanthemum	Lilac	Squash
Day lily	Mint	Violet
Dianthus	Myrtle	Yucca
English daisy	Nasturtium	

Wild Things to Gather

Ancient gatherers were well aware of the importance of the wild harvest — from cacti and yucca fruit to the tender sprouts of tumbleweed to sun-sweetened fruits and berries to herbaceous greens. These highly-valued plants sustained not only dietary needs but medicinal and ceremonial needs as well.

Amaranth	Huckleberries	Tepary beans
Cactus pads	Juniper berries	Watercress
Chiltepins	Manzanita berries	Wild grapes
Cinchweed	Mesquite pods	Wild mint
Chokeberries	Mormon tea	Wild sage
Currants	Mountain spinach	Wild spinach
Desert verbena	Rose hips	Wild strawberries
Devil's claw	Squaw berries	Young dandelions
Gauco	Tender tumbleweed	Young sorrell
Hohoise		

Resources

Kokopelli's Kitchen
Toll free 1/888-333-5859
Anasazi and Zuni Gold beans,
posole, stone-ground cornmeals,
corn husks, southwest herbs and
spices, New Mexico chile powder,
mesquite meal and pods, pine nuts
www.kokopelliskitchen.com

Maria and Juanita
P.O. Box 425
Keams Canyon, AZ 86034
Tumbleweed, culinary ash, hohoise

Genevieve Kaursgowva
P.O. Box 772
Hotevilla, AZ 86030
Piki bread, culinary ash

Winter Sun Trading Co.
928/774-2884
107 N. San Francisco St. #1
Flagstaff, AZ 86001
Tuitsma, aznafran, culinary ash

The Great Cuisine Catalog
& Spice Co.
505/323-1776
Joseph Montoya Federal Bldg.
Dept. 2514
Santa Fe, NM 87504

Casado Farms
505/852-2433
Box 1269
San Juan Pueblo, NM 87566
Dry chiles

Native Seed/SEARCH
520/622-5561
526 N. 4th Ave.
Tucson, AZ 85705
Call for catalog of over 250
seeds.

Texas Wild Game Co-op
1-800/962-GAME
P.O. Box 530
Ingram, TX 78025
Venison
www.brokenarrowranch.com

The Game Exchange
1-800/426-3872
107 Quint St.
San Francisco, CA 94124
Game
www.polarica.com

Lucky Star Ranch
607/836-4766
R.R. 1 Box 273
Chaumont, NY 13622
Game

Southwest Herbs
505/267-9368
P.O. Box 9
Arrey, NM 87930

Pecos Valley Spice Co.
P.O. Box 964
Albuquerque, NM 87103
1-800-473-8226
Masa, Southwest cookware
www.pecosvalley.com

Index

About the Authors

James and Carol Cunkle were, from 1986 through 2000, actively involved with an 800-year-old prehistoric Indian site formerly known as Raven Site Ruin. It is located in east/central Arizona on the Little Colorado River.

Anthropologist/Archaeologist James Cunkle, as the Director of the White Mountain Archaeologist Center, oversaw research, preservation and protection of Raven Site for fourteen years. Carol's operational duties included attending to the healthy appetites of the archaeologists and visitors to Raven Site. The Cunkles have become deeply involved in the traditional ways in which the prehistoric people cultivated and prepared their food.

Prehistoric seeds discovered during the excavations at Raven Site inspired an ethnobotanical garden. Many years of experimenting with the seeds, plants, and recipes collected from their Native American friends resulted in this cookbook and the product line "Kokopelli's Kitchen" (www.kokopelliskitchen.com). Questions can be directed to the Cunkles at ccunkl94@cybertrails.com

With their archaeological program concluded, the site is now under the stewardship of the Archaeological Conservancy of New Mexico (www.americanarchaeology.com.)

More Books by James R. Cunkle

STONE MAGIC of the ANCIENTS
Petroglyphs, Shamanic Shrine Sites & Ancient Rituals

James R. Cunkle and Markus A. Jacquemain examine the petroglyphs of northeastern Arizona. Story-line vignettes give the reader an insight into the lives of the area's prehistoric inhabitants. Over 400 photos and illustrations.

8 x 10 — 192 pages . . . $14.95

TREASURES OF TIME

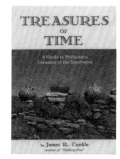

A user-friendly guide to the ceramics that have been unearthed at Raven Site Ruins in northeastern Arizona. Author James R. Cunkle categorizes the primary groups of prehistoric ceramics found at the site and treats each in a separate chapter of in-depth information. Includes color insert, glossary and index.

6 x 9 —216 pages . . . $14.95

TALKING POTS

Deciphering the Symbols of a Prehistoric People. Anthropologist/archaeologist James R. Cunkle details his experiences at Raven Site Ruin in the White Mountains of Arizona. Controversial new study of prehistoric pottery icons includes more than 200 photos and illustrations.

8 1/2 x 11—176 pages . . . $19.95

MIMBRES MYTHOLOGY
Tales from the Painted Clay

The bowls of the Mimbres Indians exhibit remarkable figurative and naturalistic images. More than 300 of these images, painted a thousand years ago, are illustrated and interpreted by author James R. Cunkle. A special bonus section features *Cachi's Story,* an enchanted tale of a young pueblo girl's rite of passage into Mimbres lore and mythology.

8 1/2 x 11—192 pages . . . $19.95

ORDER BLANK

GOLDEN WEST PUBLISHERS

☼ 4113 N. Longview Ave. • Phoenix, AZ 85014

www.goldenwestpublishers.com • **1-800-658-5830** • FAX 602-279-6901

Qty	Title	Price	Amount
	Arizona Cook Book	6.95	
	Arizona Territory Cook Book	6.95	
	Best Barbecue Recipes	6.95	
	Chili-Lovers Cook Book	6.95	
	Chip and Dip Lovers Cook Book	6.95	
	Easy Recipes for Wild Game & Fish	6.95	
	Grand Canyon Cook Book	6.95	
	Kokopelli's Cook Book	9.95	
	Mexican Family Favorites	6.95	
	Quick-n-Easy Mexican Recipes	6.95	
	Real New Mexico Chile	6.95	
	Salsa Lovers Cook Book	6.95	
	Sedona Cook Book	7.95	
	Tequila Cook Book	7.95	
	Tortilla Lovers Cook Book	6.95	
	Wholly Frijoles! The Whole Bean Cook Book	6.95	
	Mimbres Mythology	19.95	
	Stone Magic of the Ancients	14.95	
	Talking Pots	19.95	
	Treasures of Time	14.95	

Shipping & Handling Add: United States $4.00
Canada & Mexico $6.00—All others $13.00

☐ My Check or Money Order Enclosed

☐ MasterCard ☐ VISA

Total $ _____

(Payable in U.S. funds)

Acct. No. _____ Exp. Date _____

Signature _____

Name _____ Phone _____

Address _____

City/State/Zip _____

Call for a FREE catalog of all of our titles

2/04   **This order blank may be photocopied**   Koko Ck Bk